FUNNY GIRL

Music by
JULE STYNE

Lyrics by
BOB MERRILL

Book by
ISOBEL LENNART
based on her original story

Vocal Score

Price $30.00

Piano reduction by
Robert H. Noeltner

CHAPPELL & CO., INC. and WONDERFUL MUSIC CORP.

For all works contained herein:

Applications for performance of this work, whether legitimate, stock,
amateur, or foreign, should be addressed to:
TAMS-WITMARK
560 Lexington Avenue
New York, N.Y., 10022

FUNNY GIRL

Presented by RAY STARK in association with SEVEN ARTS PRODUCTIONS
First performance March 26, 1964 at the Winter Garden Theatre, New York

Directed by GARSON KANIN

Musical Numbers Staged by Carol Haney
Scenery and Lighting by Robert Randolph
Costumes Designed by Irene Sharaff
Musical Direction by Milton Rosenstock
Orchestrations by Ralph Burns
Vocal Arrangements by Buster Davis
Dance Orchestrations by Luther Henderson
Associate Producer Al Goldin
Associate Director Lawrence Kasha

Production Supervised by JEROME ROBBINS

Cast of Characters
(In order of appearance)

FANNY BRICE	Barbra Streisand
JOHN, STAGE MANAGER	Robert Howard
EMMA	Royce Wallace
MRS. BRICE	Kay Medford
MRS. STRAKOSH	Jean Stapleton
MRS. MEEKER	Lydia S. Fredericks
MRS. O'MALLEY	Joyce O'Neil
TOM KEENEY	Joseph Macaulay
EDDIE RYAN	Danny Meehan
HECKIE	Victor R. Helou
WORKMEN	Robert Howard, Robert Henson
SNUB TAYLOR	Buzz Miller
TROMBONE SMITTY	Blair Hammond
FIVE FINGER FINNEY	Alan E. Weeks
TRUMPET SOLOIST	Dick Perry
BUBBLES	Shellie Farrell
POLLY	Joan Lowe
MAUDE	Ellen Halpin
NICK ARNSTEIN	Sydney Chaplin
TWO SHOWGIRLS	Sharon Vaughn, Diana Lee Nielsen
STAGE DIRECTOR	Marc Jordan
FLORENZ ZIEGFELD, JR.	Roger De Koven
MIMSEY	Sharon Vaughn
ZIEGFELD TENOR	John Lankston
ZIEGFELD LEAD DANCER	George Reeder
ADOLPH	John Lankston
MRS. NADLER	Rose Randolf
PAUL	Larry Fuller
CATHY	Joan Cory
VERA	Lainie Kazan
JENNY	Diane Coupe
BEN	Buzz Miller
MR. RENALDI	Marc Jordan

Showgirls: Prudence Adams, Joan Cory, Diane Coupe, Lainie Kazan, Diana Lee Nielsen, Sharon Vaughn, Rosemarie Yellen.

Singers: Lydia S. Fredericks, Mary Louise, Jeanne McLaren, Joyce O'Neil, Rose Randolf, Stephanie Reynolds, Victor R. Helou, Robert Henson, Robert Howard, Marc Jordan, John Lankston, Albert Zimmerman.

Dancers: Edie Cowan, Christine Dalsey, Shellie Farrell, Ellen Halpin, Rosemary Jelincic, Karen Kristin, Joan Lowe, Jose Ahumada, Bud Fleming, Larry Fuller, Blair Hammond, John Nola, Alan Peterson, Alan E. Weeks.

FUNNY GIRL

Synopsis of Scenes

THE TIME: Shortly before and after World War I.

ACT I

SCENE 1: Fanny's Dressing Room — The New Amsterdam Theatre

SCENE 2: Backstage — Keeney's Music Hall

SCENE 3: In Front of Keeney's Music Hall

SCENE 4: Backyard — Fanny's Neighborhood

SCENE 5: Onstage — Keeney's Music Hall

SCENE 6: Backstage and Chorus Dressing Room
Immediately following

SCENE 7: Mrs. Brice's Kitchen

SCENE 8: Backstage — The New York Theatre

SCENE 9: Onstage — The New York Theatre

SCENE 10: In Front of Follies Curtain
Immediately following

SCENE 11: Henry Street

SCENE 12: Interior of Mrs. Brice's Saloon

SCENE 13: A Private Dining Room — Baltimore

SCENE 14: Baltimore Railroad Terminal

ACT II

SCENE 1: The Arnstein Long Island Mansion

SCENE 2: Mrs. Brice's Saloon

SCENE 3: Backstage — The New Amsterdam Theatre
Circa 1920

SCENE 4: Onstage — The New Amsterdam Theatre

SCENE 5: Fanny's Dressing Room
Immediately following

SCENE 6: Study — The Arnstein House

SCENE 7: Backstage — The New Amsterdam Theatre

SCENE 8: Onstage — The New Amsterdam Theatre

SCENE 9: Fanny's Dressing Room — The New Amsterdam Theatre

Instrumentation

Woodwind No. 1: Alto Saxophone/Clarinet/Flute/Alto Flute/Piccolo

No. 2: Alto Saxophone/Clarinet/Flute/Piccolo/Soprano Saxophone

No. 3: Tenor Saxophone/Clarinet/Bass Clarinet

No. 4: Tenor Saxophone/Clarinet/Oboe/English Horn

No. 5: Bass Saxophone/Bassoon/Bass Clarinet

Horn, 3 Trumpets, 3 Trombones, Percussion, Guitar, Piano/Celesta

6 Violins, 3 Violoncellos, Contrabass

Musical Program

ACT I

ACT II

FUNNY GIRL
Overture

No. 1

Lyrics by
BOB MERRILL

Music by
JULE STYNE

Attacca

Opening - Act I
(Underscore)

Piano

No. 3

Poker Chant No. 1

Cue: EMMA takes Indian costume out of closet.

Piano

MRS. BRICE: think so? I think so. You with your glass face, I think you got noth-ing.

Sar-ah Stra-kosh, you have-n't got a sec-ond ace! __ MRS.STRAKOSH: Then my ad-

vice to you is, hon-ey__ Close up your mouth And put up the mon-ey!

Cls. Vlns. pizz. Trbs. *pp* Hn.,Trbs.

Segue as one

No.4

If A Girl Isn't Pretty

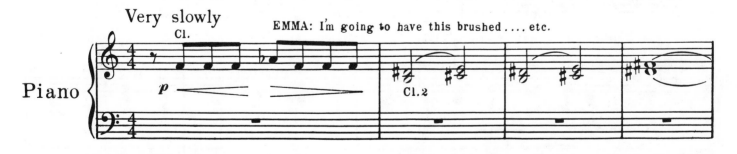

Very slowly
Cl.

EMMA: I'm going to have this brushed....etc.

Piano

p Cl.2

KEENEY: You're fired!

Repeat until cue: KEENEY:
A great choice for the chorus, Eddie.

Slowly

What's the matter .. you owe

somebody a favor? etc.....

FANNY: I've been on the stage since I was ten.... etc.

Cue: FANNY:
But Mr. Keeney! --
EDDIE:

If a

I'm The Greatest Star

When I ex - pose it! Can't you see to look at me That I'm

a natch - ral "Ca - mille." As Ca - mille I just feel

I've so much to of - fer. I know I'd be di - vine be - cause

I'm a nat - u - ral cough - er,

Dixieland

i'm the great-est, great-est star!

Trb. gliss *ff* Tutti (*notation ad lib.*)

No. 5a   Change Of Scene

Cue. **FANNY:** Follow me.

Moderately - In 2

[Scene changes to backyard]

Piano

f Br. W.W.

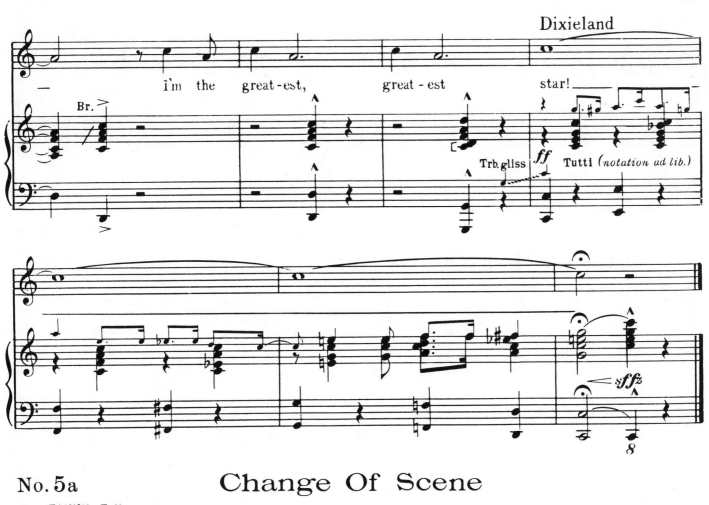

Fade out as lights come up.

No.5b   I'm The Greatest Star - Reprise

Cue: FANNY: Mama!

No.6   Eddie's Fifth Encore

Moderately - In 4

No.6a   Chaser

Piano

No.7 # Cornet Man

Cue: EDDIE: Hit it, Professor!

-il that's worse._ Yes, a horn's my thorn, He's a trav-lin' cor-net man._

Faster

147 DANCERS:
Chick, chick-en scram - ble. Chick, chick-en scram-

- ble. Chick, chick-en scram - ble.

49

attacca

No. 7a

Cornet Man-Chaser

Piano

[Scene changes to backstage]

Faster

+Trb., Bs. Sax.

Fade out as EDDIE speaks.

Cl.

Tpts.

etc.

Dr.
ad lib.

Nicky Arnstein No.1

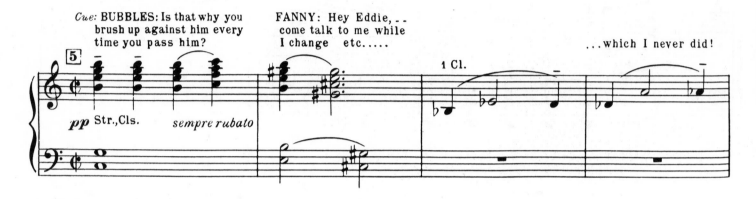

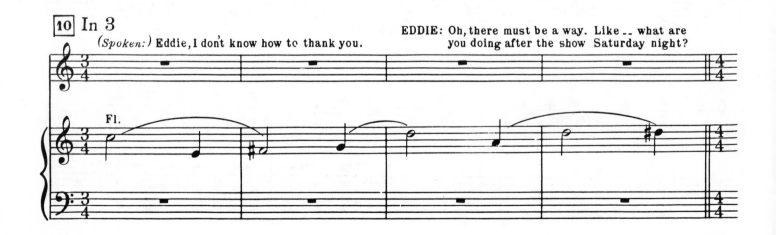

Change Of Scene
(If A Girl Isn't Pretty)

No. 10 Who Taught Her Everything?

Cue: MRS. STRAKOSH: Fanny, darling, tell me everything.

who used to stand there And feed her the seed? Who taught her how to pick her

MRS. BRICE: That I did, Eddie. *(Taps)*

clothes? Who taught her how to tap her toes?

But will she ad-mit it? Kid, you said it. They all for-get they know ya when it

comes to cred-it. Tell me, have you ev-er seen her take this pose?_

I taught her ev'ry-thing, How to hoof and how to sing. I taught her ev'ry-thing she

knows.

MRS. BRICE: *Wait, Eddie, she'll blame us yet.*

49 MRS. B: EDDIE: *Let me hear it, Rosie.*

Who taught her ev-'ry-thing she knows?   I taught her ev-'ry-thing she

knows.

EDDIE: *Ain't it the truth!*

knows.   The mis-chie-vous smile, That dev-il may care. You

We taught her ev-'ry-thing she knows.

Attacca

No. 10a

Change Of Scene
(I'm The Greatest Star)

Piano

[Fade out as director calls up to Mr. Ziegfeld]

No. 10b

End Of Scene 8

Cue: FANNY exits in head-dress.

Slow drag - In 4 *[Scene changes to stage of New York Theatre]*

Piano

Attacca

His Love Makes Me Beautiful

rav-ish-ing-ly? With - in the se-cret heart of ev'ry bride

These are the words re - peat-ing, re-peat-ing, re-peat-ing in -

side. You are the

beau-ti-ful re-flec-tion Of his love's af-fec-tion, A walk-ing il-lus-tra-tion

26 Gracefully

Of his a-do-ra-tion. His love makes you beau-ti-ful, So beau-ti-ful So beau-ti-ful. You ask your

34 SHOWGIRLS:

Ooh_____ Ooh_____ Ooh_____

look-ing glass,What is it_ makes you so ex-quis-ite? The an-swer to your que-ry_

No. 11a

Change Of Scene

No. 12 I Want To Be Seen With You Tonight

Cue: NICK: ....watch people stare and whisper ..

proximity Gives rumors to rise. We'll let them analyze— What our amalgamation implies! Oh, yes, The gossips will press, Too willing to stress

Nicky Arnstein No. 2

Cue: **NICK:** Now hurry and get changed ‑‑ go on!

Nick‑y Arn‑stein, Nick‑y Arn‑stein, What a beau‑ti‑ful, beau‑ti‑ful name!

Wait till he meets in per‑son, For one night on‑ly,— Mis‑sus

Stra‑kosh and the Hen‑ry Street gyp‑sys.— I'll nev‑er see him a‑gain.

[Dance]

63 W.W., Vlns. stacc.

f Br., Glock.
Hn., Celli

+ Tuba

Tpts.
Trb., Celli

(p)

Tpts.
Hn., Celli

(p)

71

(Glock. tacet)

Hn.

Tpts.

3

3

3

79 ALL:

We're proud to tell you that C. P. A.'s We got in

W.W., Str., Glock.

mf

Trbs.

Zieg - feld ——— star! ———

No. 14a Music Under Dialogue
(Henry Street)

NICK: Mrs. Brice __ you must be very proud .... etc.

Moderately

Piano

Repeat and fade out at cue: MRS. STRAKOSH: Excuse me, girls.

People

Cue: **FANNY:** then you'd really see a fuss! Funny

[Applause]

in the world.

Gtr. solo *ff* Tutti *ff*

+Timp. attacca

No. 15a

Poker Chant No. 2

Moderately - In 4

[Scene changes to MRS. BRICE'S saloon]

Piano

f Tutti   Dr.   Dr.

Ad lib.

MRS. BRICE:

I think you're bluff-ing, Mis-sus

p   rall.   Str *fz* > *p*   +Trb.

MRS. STRAKOSH: MRS. BRICE: Spoken:
No. I don't....etc.

Stra-kosh,   Bluff-ing!   You   think so?___   I   think   so!

No. 16
End Of Scene 12

Cue: MRS. BRICE: Take it. I thought you were bluffing.

[*Fade out as curtain rises and segue to No. 17*]

attacca

No. 17 Incidental

Private dining room scene.

[*PAUL is placing white roses on table and awaiting the arrival of NICK ARNSTEIN*]

No.18 You Are Woman, I Am Man

Cue: NICK: I'll be much more direct!

Attacca

No. 18a

Change Of Scene

[*The scene changes to the Baltimore Railroad Station.*]

Moderately bright - In 2

Piano

Don't Rain On My Parade

Cue: **FANNY: If you mean it later, I'll be sorry!**

I'll march my band out,— I'll beat my drum. And if I'm fanned out,— Your turn at bat, sir,— At least, I did-n't fake it. Hat, sir!— I guess I did-n't make it! Get read-y for me,—

Tempo I°

love,'Cause I'm a "com - er".   I   sim - ply got - ta___ march, My heart's a drum-mer.

Allargando - In 4

No - bod - y, no,__ no - bod - y   Is gon - na   rain on my pa -

93 Tempo Iº

rade!

End Act I

No. 20

Entr'acte

Moderately bright waltz - In 1

No. 21

Sadie, Sadie

Cue: VERA: Tell me.. what's it like.. being married, Fanny?

FANNY: Fanny?

Moderately slow - In 4

Sa - die, Sa - die, mar - ried la - dy, Bow when I go by._

I'm a cor - por - a - tion now,_ Not

me, my - self and I. Oh, how that mar - riage li - cense works_ On

No. 21a

Change Of Scene
(If A Girl Isn't Pretty)

No. 22

Find Yourself A Man

Cue: MRS. BRICE: I don't have to worry about them any more__

Change Of Scene
(Rat - tat - tat - tat)

No. 23

Rat-tat-tat-tat

Cue: **EDDIE:** This show opens in four and a half weeks.

ev - 'ry - thing that you would do _____ And more!

39

EDDIE:

Rat - tat - tat - tat, We'll give their backs a big pat.__ They de-

serve a fu - ture full of joys,_____ 'Cause they're our

47

Yan - kee Doo - dle, Yan - kee Doo - dle,

Yan - kee Doo - dle dough - boys.

No. 23a

Rat - tat - tat - tat - Part 2
(Private Schwartz)

Listesso tempo

JENNY and Company:

Com - pa - ny__   Or- der__   Arms!

Piano

f + Trbs.

SOLO VOICE:

Roll   call!   I'm   pri - vate Jones from Ar - kan - sas,   I'm

Tutti

Vlns. trem.

mp

Cello

+ Rds., Trbs.__

etc.

Segue as one

Attacca

No. 23b

Change Of Scene

Brightly - In 2

Piano

[Fade out as curtain rises]

No. 24   # Who Are You Now?

Cue. FANNY: No, It's not all right.

some-one bet-ter for my love?_____ +Tpts.

Fl. 8va

rall.

poco accel.

ff

Attacca

No. 24a ## Change Of Scene

Maestoso - In 4

Tpts.

Piano

ff Tutti

rall. molto

No. 25 ## Don't Rain On My Parade
(Nick's Version)

Cue: NICK: It's all right. Forget it!

NICK: Beekman 4119....

Hold until NICK hangs up phone.

Moderately bright - In 2

1 Vln.

ppp

2d Vln.

Cello

Br., Cls.
mf

NICK:

One roll for the whole she - bang! One throw__that bell will go

Cls.

Str.

Cls.

p Hn. growl

Hn. growl

clang! This time we play with my deck! Out of my way—it's my

neck! This time the set-up feels right! Ba-by, it's o-pen-ing

night! Hey, Miss-us Arn-stein, Here I go! _____

No. 26

Opening Scene 7
(Downtown Rag)

[Scene changes to New Amsterdam Theatre — bare stage rehearsal.]

Moderately bright - In 2

No. 27   The Music That Makes Me Dance

Cue: **FANNY** *is alone at work-table. The lights dim.*

Piano

2 Ad lib.

Piano only

I add two and two.. The most sim-ple ad-di-tion, Then

swear that the fig-ures are ly-ing. I'm a much bet-ter com-ic than

math-e-ma-ti-cian 'Cause I'm bet-ter on stage than at in-ter-mis-sion. And as

far as the man is con-cerned.. If I've been burned, I have-n't

VOICE: *(over loudspeaker)* Ladies and gentlemen, Florenz Ziegfeld
presents the one and only Fanny Brice!

Slowly - In tempo

learned.

[Orch.]

Cls., Str. (Celesta)

16 Moderately slow 4

know he's a-round when the sky and the ground start in ring-ing.

Cls., Str.

I know when he's near by the thun-der I hear in ad-

Alto Sax.

24

His words and his words a-lone are the

vance.
Alto solo

Str., W.W.

mu - sic that makes me dance!

No. 27a

Change Of Scene
(The Music That Makes Me Dance)

Moderately - In 4

Piano

No. 28 # Incidental - Underscore

Cue: **FANNY: Come in.**

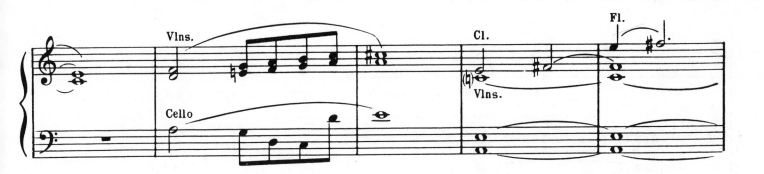

No. 29

Finale - Act II
(Don't Rain On My Parade - Reprise)

Cue· FANNY *picks the blue marble egg.*

Life's can - dy and the ___ sun's a ball of but - ter.

Don't bring ___ a - round a cloud to rain on my pa -

rade! ___

Str., Xyl.
+Br.
f

20 Più mosso

I'm gon - na live and live now! Get what I

Str.
W.W.
+Str.

want; I know how! All that the law will al-

Hn. growl

28 Slowly - In 4

low! Hey, gor-geous, here we go a - gain! ____

Saxs., Str.

f +Br.

34 Più mosso

Yes, here it goes, kid, —

Saxs.

Str. sust.

fz > p

mp

Trbs.

Str., Saxs.

Tpts.

No look - ing back.

Curtain and Exit Music